THIS IS THE STORY OF
INDEPENDENCE DAY,
THE FOURTH OF JULY

THE
Fourth of July Story

by ALICE DALGLIESH

Illustrated by MARIE NONNAST

ALADDIN PAPERBACKS

Second Aladdin Paperbacks edition 1995
First Aladdin Books edition 1987
Copyright © 1956 by Alice Dalgliesh and Marie Nonnast
Aladdin Paperbacks
An imprint of Simon & Schuster
Children's Publishing Division
1230 Avenue of the Americas
New York, NY 10020
Manufactured in China
30 29

Library of Congress Cataloging-in-Publication Data
Dalgliesh, Alice, date.
The Fourth of July story / by Alice Dalgliesh ; illustrated by Marie Nonnast.
— 2nd Aladdin Paperbacks ed.
p.   cm.
ISBN 978-0-689-71876-2
1. Fourth of July—Juvenile literature.   2. United States. Declaration of Independence—
Juvenile literature.   3. United States—History—Revolution, 1775–1783—
Juvenile literature.   I. Nonnast, Marie.   II. Title.   III. Title: 4th of July story.
[E221.D14 1995]
973.3'13—dc20   94-29290

1120 SCP

AUTHOR'S NOTE

THE STORY of the birthday of our country is a big story to tell young children. Yet when they begin to ask, ''Why do we have a holiday on the Fourth of July?'' they have a right to know. They have a right to know that Independence Day is something more than fireworks and picnics.

In telling the story I have used few names and tried to give only a few clear impressions. I have not indicated, therefore, the exact chronology. Older children may learn that Richard Henry Lee's resolution was voted on July 2nd, the Declaration on July 4th, and that all the states did not sign until August. For younger children it is all ''The Fourth of July.''

The Birthday
of Our Country

IT was the Fourth of July in the city of Philadelphia more than two hundred years ago.

Children who lived near the State House must have seen the candles lighted there on that stormy afternoon. Something wonderful was happening in Philadelphia this fourth day of July in 1776. It was the birthday of our country.

After that, the children were often to hear the voice of the bell that hung in the tower of the State House. Once it even woke them at three o'clock in the morning!

And always the bell seemed to say:

"Liberty throughout the land,
Liberty to all the people!"

The Story of Freedom

THIS was how it happened. This is why the Liberty Bell spoke to the people.

Our country was not always the big nation it is now. The land was there and the rivers and the mountains, the lakes and the forests. Part of it still belonged to the Indians, who lived here for a long, long time. Part of it had been settled by people from Britain and from other countries across the ocean.

On the east coast there were thirteen colonies that belonged to Britain. Each one was like a little separate country. Each had its own name. Virginia was the place where the first Englishmen had landed and made their homes. The Pilgrims had landed in Massachusetts.

There came a time when some of the thirteen colonies did not want to belong to Britain, or to the English king. They did not think that men across the sea should make any laws, or rules, for them.

They wanted to make all their own laws, to be free and independent. So they began to feel more like one country instead of thirteen colonies, but it was still some time before they would learn that they must all work together.

People came together in many places to talk about being free and independent.

On some village greens they raised Liberty poles as a sign that they wanted freedom.

MASSACHUSETTS (MAINE DISTRICT)

NEW HAMPSHIRE

MASSACHUSETTS

RHODE ISLAND

NEW YORK

CONNECTICUT

PENNSYLVANIA

NEW JERSEY

DELAWARE

MARYLAND

VIRGINIA

N. CAROLINA

INDIAN COUNTRY

S. CAROLINA

GEORGIA

ATLANTIC OCEAN

Men made fiery speeches that everyone remembered. In the colony of Virginia, Patrick Henry made a speech that ended, "Give me liberty or give me death!" No one could forget those words.

The English king wanted to keep his American colonies. Many people in the American colonies still wanted to belong to Britain. Some of the leaders on both sides tried hard to work things out so that there would not be war. But at last the king sent warships and soldiers to the city of Boston. The first shots were fired at Lexington and Concord, in Massachusetts.

Now the thirteen colonies knew they *must* work together. Men from all the colonies came riding to a meeting in the State House in Philadelphia. They called themselves ''The Congress,'' because congress means ''coming together.''

It was a wonderful day when Richard Henry Lee of Virginia stood before the Congress and said that ''These United Colonies are . . . free and independent States.''

A general had to be chosen to lead the army, so the Congress chose Colonel George Washington of Virginia. ''A gentleman from Virginia, well-known to all of us.''

Tall, serious George Washington, in his handsome uniform, told the Congress that he was proud to be chosen. Then he went to take command of the army.

The men who represented the thirteen colonies talked a long time and thought a long time, trying to decide whether they could be free and independent states. There was thoughtful talk and angry talk, but they were beginning to agree.

They chose a committee of five men to write down the things they believed in, and all the reasons why they had wanted to be free. It would be a DECLARATION OF INDEPENDENCE.

Writing the Declaration

THE committee asked a young man named Thomas Jefferson to do the writing. Thomas Jefferson came from the proud and beautiful colony of Virginia, with its red soil and tall blue mountains. He was not a good speaker, but he loved to write.

It was a very big thing to do, but Thomas Jefferson was willing to try it. So, using the plain little wooden desk that he liked to write on, he began. All day, and part of each night, he sat in his rooms in a three-story brick house, writing. Often he crossed out one word and put in another.

The other men on the committee read what Thomas Jefferson had written and gave him advice. Wise old Benjamin Franklin of Philadelphia made suggestions. So did sturdy John Adams of Massachusetts, who had worked hard for freedom.

But when the Declaration of Independence was finished, most of the words were Thomas Jefferson's.

They were wonderful words that said the United States of America had the right to form their own government. This government was to be chosen by the people. If it was not a good government, the people had the right to say so and to change it.

There were more wonderful words that said that all men were "created equal," that all of them had a right to "life, liberty and the pursuit of happiness." To live in their own country, to be free to do the things that they believed in, the things that they hoped would make them happy. What more could men want?

Now the work was done, but all men from the thirteen states had to decide that the words Thomas Jefferson had written were true and good and fair. Once again there was thoughtful talk and angry talk. Thomas Jefferson sat and listened. It was not easy for him to sit there as the Congress made changes in the Declaration.

Then the names of the states were called and men from each state said, "I vote for Independence"—or voted against it.

When the men from all the states had agreed, they signed their names. John Hancock, the president of the

Congress, was the first to sign. He always wrote his name in big, bold letters, but on the Declaration he wrote it even larger:

The story is told that on the Fourth of July a boy had been waiting all day to give a signal to an old bell-ringer up in the tower. And when Congress had voted on the Declaration of Independence, the boy called ''RING! RING!''

Then the bell-ringer pulled on the ropes and the Liberty Bell rang out:

> Liberty throughout the land,
> Liberty to all the people.

A few days later, on July the eighth, the Liberty Bell rang again to call the people of Philadelphia together.

Many of them came to the State House, down the narrow streets, past the red brick houses. Some stayed at home because they still wanted to belong to Britain. Some did not think there should be war. Some had read the news in their newspapers. But in the yard of the State House, which later was called Independence Hall, those who came heard the Declaration of Independence read aloud.

As the reader finished, the people cheered.

The Liberty Bell rang out, and all the bells in the city were set to ringing. They rang all day and kept on ringing as the stars came out in the night sky.

Liberty throughout the land,
Liberty to all the people.

To Carry the News

THE news had to go to all the thirteen states. Copies of the Declaration had been printed in Philadelphia, in a little printing shop, on the night of the Fourth of July.

No telephone, no telegraph, no radio, no television to take the news. No trains, no automobiles, no airplanes to carry the Declaration of Independence. How did it travel?

Men on horseback carried the news. They put the printed copies of the Declaration in their saddlebags.

They rode far and they rode fast, over rough roads. Over mountains they rode, over shaky little bridges, or splashing through streams that had no bridges. And when one horse was tired, there was another waiting, for the news must go on and on—and on.

All through the country the riders went, taking the news that the Liberty Bell had told—

> Liberty throughout the land,
> Liberty to all the people.

Some people heard the news in church. Perhaps the minister read the words of the Liberty Bell just as they were engraved on the bell—for they come from the Bible and sound like the deep tones of the bell itself:

> ''Proclaim liberty throughout all the land,
>   Unto all the inhabitants thereof.''

Then the minister said, ''God bless the United States of America. Let all the people say Amen.''

''Amen,'' said the voices of the fathers and mothers and the small voices of the children.

Perhaps, as a rider went through the rich farm lands of Pennsylvania, he stopped to rest his horse, or to tell the news to a friend who was a farmer.

Then the farmer stopped work to listen and to think about this wonderful thing that had happened.

The farmer wasn't British like many of the people in the colonies. He spoke German. His people had come to America to be free to worship God in their own way. Now this was his own country—THE UNITED STATES OF AMERICA.

The rider went on and the sound of the horse's hoofs grew fainter and fainter. But the farmer still thought about the news. This was his farm, his land; he would always be free to do the work he had chosen to do.

There was one messenger who had to carry the news from Philadelphia to New York, riding as swiftly as he could. He was taking a copy of the Declaration of Independence to George Washington. The general was in New York because the British ships were expected to attack the city.

When the news came, the general ordered the Declaration to be read to the soldiers. Now they knew that they were fighting for their own country:

THE UNITED STATES OF AMERICA.

The Declaration ended with the ringing words that Thomas Jefferson had written:

''And for the support of this Declaration we . . . pledge to each other our lives, our fortunes and our sacred honour.''

Before very long many of those soldiers would give their lives for their country.

But at that time they were gay and full of excitement. They pulled down a statue of King George the Third, of Great Britain. It should be melted, they said, and made into bullets for their guns. General Washington did not approve of this. He thought the people should celebrate in an orderly way.

All over the country the people were excited and they were not always orderly. They went through the streets carrying pictures and figures of the king, and threw them on fires they had made. Bonfires blazed, bells rang, people cheered and shouted.

Some of them came together at the Liberty poles they had put up before, to hear the Declaration read. Some gathered under a Liberty tree, where they had held their meetings to talk about independence.

Our soldiers had scarcely enough gunpowder for their cannon, but in some places guns and cannon were fired thirteen times, once for each of the thirteen states.

These thirteen states made up the first United States of America, the first thirteen stars in the American flag. Later, other states would join them and there would be more stars in the flag.

It took a long time for the Declaration of Independence to travel to all the thirteen states. It was two months before it came to the states far down in the South.

In one small settlement on the border between the states of North and South Carolina, there lived a boy named Andrew Jackson. At that time many people did not know how to read, but Andy Jackson had been to school, and he had been able to read since he was five years old. Now he was nine and could even read the newspaper to people of the little town.

So when a copy of the Declaration of Independence arrived, a group of people came eagerly together to hear Andrew Jackson read it. He had to practice it first, so that when the time came he could read it clearly, and not stop to spell out the long words.

He began: ''In Congress, July 4, 1776

A Declaration by the Representatives of the United States of America''

He was only a boy with freckles and sandy hair that never seemed to stay in place. No one could have guessed that some day he would be the seventh president of the United States of America.

ALL this time, while the news was being carried, and for several years after that, the American Revolution, or war for freedom, went on. General Washington was leading his army. It was a hard war, and sometimes our soldiers were cold and hungry. Sometimes they had only ragged clothes to wear, no uniforms, and no shoes for their feet. And many of the soldiers were only boys, fifteen years old.

Sometimes it seemed as if the British soldiers, in their fine red coats, would win the war. They won battles and captured towns and cities.

When the British were coming to Philadelphia, the Liberty Bell was taken down from its tower. It was hidden under the floor of a church so that no enemy soldiers could find it.

The Congress had to move from Philadelphia to another city—and another—and another. Always, the Declaration of Independence went with them. The Declaration was taken to many different places. Once it even spent the night in a barn.

It was a dark and sad time for the United States of America. But some of the countries across the sea in Europe sent help.

One day a young French general named Lafayette landed in America. He brought the news that ships and soldiers were coming from France to join the Americans in their fight for liberty. Even brave General Washington had tears in his eyes when he heard this wonderful news.

Soon the French arrived, and this helped a great deal.

At last the war was over, and the United States of America had won it. The battle that decided the war was fought in the state of Virginia. Some of the first words about Independence had come from Virginia, and there, on the battlefield of Yorktown, the British surrendered to General Washington. They gave up their flags and put their guns on the ground. When the news reached Philadelphia the Liberty Bell rang at three o'clock in the morning.

Not long after this Britain agreed that the United States had a right to be free, and that they were a new nation. As time went on, Britain and America became friends. Many people in Britain had not wanted the war at all.

The soldiers went back to their homes and their wives and their children. The Liberty Bell was taken back to its tower in Philadelphia.

The states still had not learned to work together as one nation. They needed a strong leader. And so George Washington was chosen by the people to be the first president of the United States of America. John Adams, who had helped with the Declaration of Independence, was the second president. Thomas Jefferson, who had written it, was the third.

Independence Day, the Fourth of July, became our most important national holiday.

Now the Declaration of Independence is in the city of Washington, where many children and grownups go to see it.

The Liberty Bell is in a room in Independence Hall in the city of Philadelphia. It is a very old bell, and it is cracked and cannot ring any more. But it is still a very wonderful bell, and on it we may read the words:

"Proclaim liberty throughout all the land,
Unto all the inhabitants thereof."